The Parrot Book

PARROTS and OTHER EXOTIC BIRDS

By Tibor Gergely

GOLDEN PRESS • NEW YORK
Western Publishing Company, Inc.
Racine, Wisconsin

© 1965 by Western Publishing Company, Inc. All rights reserved. Produced in U.S.A. GOLDEN, A GOLDEN SHAPE BOOK®, and GOLDEN PRESS® are trademarks of Western Publishing Company, Inc. No part of this book may be reproduced or copied in any form without written permission from the publisher.

Special GOLDENCRAFT® Edition

Macaws are large, noisy members of the parrot family.

They have feathers of many colors.

This big, beautiful bird is a parrot.

Parrots that live with people sometimes learn to talk.

Cockatoos are parrots, too.

They live for many years.

Parakeets are tiny parrots.

They come in many colors.

The peacock is one

of the handsomest birds of all.

Toucans' bills
are almost bigger
than their bodies.

This is an upside-down bird-of-paradise.

He is showing off for his mate.

The baby wood ducks are learning to swim with their mother.
The mandarin duck is watching them.

Both brown and white pelicans can hold many fish in the pouches under their bills.

Bright-colored flamingos dip their beaks under water to get food.

During the time when they nest, flamingos live in large flocks.

Pretty little canaries are fine singers.
People often keep canaries as pets.

When the baby penguin grows up, he will be black and white like his parents.